StartUp Reading 2

Gina Kim and Carolyn S. Hyatt

WorldCom Edu

Gina Kim and Carolyn S. Hyatt

© 2006 published by WorldCom Edu.

Cover/Interior Design: Design Nalgae
Illustrations: Wishing Star

ISBN: 89-8127-620-X

Desk Copy Request / Information
To place your desk copy request or for more information, please contact the following office:
Tel: (02) 3273-4300   Fax: (02) 3273-4303
Homepage : www.wcbooks.co.kr

Contents

1 How Animals Live

 **Before You Read**

1. Where can you find sand?
2. Do you like to play with sand?
3. Look at the picture. Is the place hot or cold?

Many animals live in sandy places. Some sandy places are very hot. It is too hot for animals to **move during** the day. The animals **wait** until it is dark to **find** food. They look for food and water. It rains very little in sandy places. **Sometimes** there is no water. But animals find water in plants. So animals know how to live in sandy places. Aren't they clever?

Word Match

Match each word with the correct meaning.

1. **during**		a.	not all the time
2. **wait**		b.	through the whole time
3. **move**		c.	to go from one place to another
4. **find**		d.	to stay in a place
5. **sometimes**		e.	to look for something

✳ Reading Comprehension

Choose the correct word.

1. This story is about animals that live in ________.

   a. sand   b. cold places   c. sandy places

2. When it is ________, the animals look for water in sandy

   places.

   a. cloudy   b. raining   c. dark

3. The animals find water in ________.

   a. rocks   b. plants   c. sand

4. You can tell that these animals get food and water ________.

   a. at night   b. in the rain   c. during the day

✳ General Understanding

Circle T for true or F for false.

1. Some sandy places are cold.   T   F

2. When it is light, the animals come out.   T   F

3. It rains very little in sandy places.   T   F

4. Animals find water in plants.   T   F

✳ Word Practice

A Circle the correct word.

1. I can't _______ my bag.   [find | look]

2. Can you help me _______ the box?   [move | wait]

3. I don't like to wait in the _______.   [sky | dark]

4. I can't _______ to go back to school.   [wait | help]

5. _______ at the beautiful sky.   [See | Look]

B Choose the right word from the box below.

move	wait	sometimes	live

1. Many animals _______ in sandy places.

2. It is too hot to _______.

3. The animals _______ until it is dark.

4. _______ there is no water.

✳ Picture Comprehension

Circle the picture of a sandy place.

a b c d

✳ Summary & Listening Practice

SUR2-1-02
MP3

Some sandy places are hot. It is very hot ①_______ the day.
Animals can't ②_______ during the day. The animals ③_______
until it is dark to ④_______ food. Sometimes there is no water in
sandy places. It is difficult to live in ⑤_______ places.

 2 Night Workers

Before You Read

SUR2-2-03
MP3

1. What time do you go to b
2. What do you do before you go to bed?
3. Do you know someone who works at night?

Many people work at night. These
people sleep during the day.
They have many different **jobs**.
Some people **cook** food at night.
Some people **fix** roads at night.
Some people take care of **sick** people.
Others put out fires. Sometimes it is **hard** to work at night.
But these people are happy to do their jobs. Why? Because
they know the city needs them.

Word Match

Match each word with the correct meaning.

1. **sick**   a. to heat food before eating it
2. **cook**   b. the work that someone is paid
                          to do
3. **job**   c. not healthy
4. **fix**   d. not easy
5. **hard**   e. to repair something

✳ Reading Comprehension

Choose the correct word.

1. This story is about _______.

    a. night   b. sleeping

    c. people who work at night

2. At night, some people fix _______.

    a. roads   b. windows   c. hospitals

3. Sometimes people find it _______ to work at night.

    a. easy   b. fun   c. hard

4. You can tell that there is a lot of work to do _______.

    a. during the day   b. at night   c. at noon

✳ General Understanding

Circle T for true or F for false.

1. Few people work at night.   T F

2. Some people cook food at night.   T F

3. Some people put out fires when it is dark.   T F

4. It is easy to work at night.   T F

A Circle the correct word.

1. My brother is _______ today. He has a cold.

   [well ǀ sick]

2. Can you _______ the chair?　　　　[fix ǀ cook]

3. It is too noisy outside. I can't _______.　　[sleep ǀ wake up]

4. My parents _______ at a bakery.　　[work ǀ listen]

5. Sometimes it is _______ to wake up early.

   [night ǀ hard]

B Choose the right word from the box below.

jobs	hard	work	fix

1. Many people _______ at night.

2. There are many different _______.

3. Some people _______ roads.

4. Sometimes it is _______ to work at night.

✳ Picture Comprehension

Choose the picture that goes with the sentence.

Circle the picture of a fire fighter.

a   b   c   d

✳ Summary & Listening Practice

SUR2-2-04
MP3

Listen and fill in the blanks.

Some people work at night. They have many ①_______. Some people take care of ②_______ people or cook food. Others ③_______ the roads. Sometimes it is ④_______ to work at night. But they are ⑤_______ to do their jobs because the city needs them.

3 To See Well

 **Before You Read**

SUR2-3-05
MP3

1. Do you wear glasses?
2. Can you see well without glasses?
3. Do you know someone who wears glasses?

Some people can't see or **read** well. **Light** comes **through** our eyes. We see a **picture** made by the light. The picture is not **clear** for some people. Glasses make the picture clearer. They are very important to these people. Without glasses, these people can't see well. So they wear glasses all the time.

Word Match

Match each word with the correct meaning.

1. **light**   a. from one side to the other

2. **read**   b. something that shines

3. **picture**   c. easy to see

4. **through**   d. an image of something

5. **clear**   e. to look at written words

✳ Reading Comprehension

Choose the correct word.

1. This story is about ________.
    a. reading   b. books   c. people who wear glasses

2. Light makes a ________.
    a. circle   b. picture   c. square

3. Glasses help people ________ well.
    a. see   b. walk   c. run

4. You can tell that these people need glasses ________.
    a. when they eat   b. only at night   c. all the time

✳ General Understanding

Circle T for true or F for false.

1. Everyone can read well.   T   F

2. Light makes a picture.   T   F

3. Glasses help a person to read.   T   F

4. Glasses are very important to some people.   T   F

✳ Word Practice

A Circle the correct word.

1. Light comes _______ the window.   [through | back]

2. I like to _______ many books.   [read | ride]

3. The sky is _______ today.   [clever | clear]

4. I can't see anything without my _______.

          [glasses | classes]

5. Let's _______ the old man.   [help | fix]

B Choose the right word from the box below.

clear	help	read	pictures

1. Some people can't _______ without their glasses.

2. We see _______ made by light.

3. The picture is not _______ for some people.

4. Glasses _______ a person to see.

☀ Picture Comprehension

Choose the picture that goes with the sentence.

Circle the picture of a person who needs glasses.

a

b

c

d

☀ Summary & Listening Practice

Listen and fill in the blanks.

SUR2-3-06
MP3

Light comes ①_______ our eyes and makes a ②_______. We see the picture made by the ③_______. Some people can't see or ④_______ well because the picture is not ⑤_______. Glasses ⑥_______ the picture become clearer.

4 Spring Fun

 ## Before You Read

1. What do you like to do on a spring day?
2. Do you know what a kite looks like?
3. Can you make a kite?

Children like to fly kites in the **spring**. Some kites are big, others are small. Kites **also** come in **pretty** colors. They fly **high** in the sky. You can see them go up and down. The **wind** helps them fly in the sky. You cannot fly a kite without the wind. Do you know that the wind also makes kites go from side to side? So fly a kite and have fun!

Word Match

Match each word with the correct meaning.

1. **spring**   a. the time of the year between winter and summer

2. **also**   b. a strong movement of air

3. **pretty**   c. a long way up

4. **wind**   d. nice to look at

5. **high**   e. too; added to

 Reading Comprehension

Choose the correct word.

1. This story is about _______.

   a. spring   b. children   c. kites

2. Children like to fly kites on _______ days.

   a. cloudy   b. spring   c. rainy

3. Kites go up and down because of the _______.

   a. wind   b. sun   c. rain

4. You can tell that kites can't fly if there is no _______.

   a. wind   b. rain   c. snow

General Understanding

Circle T for true or F for false.

1. Children don't like to fly kites.   T   F

2. Children like to fly kites in the spring.   T   F

3. Kites come in pretty colors.   T   F

4. Rain helps kites go up and down.   T   F

☀ Word Practice

A Circle the correct word.

1. The rainbow has many _______ colors.   [pretty | same]

2. The birds fly _______ in the sky.   [high | sit]

3. Some people live in _______ houses.   [angry | big]

4. I like to climb _______ mountains.   [up | cup]

5. In the _______, you can see many flowers.

[spring | winter]

B Choose the right word from the box below.

sky	kites	spring	wind

1. Children like to fly kites in the _______.

2. Some _______ are big.

3. Kites go up and down in the _______.

4. Kites can fly because of the _______.

✳ Picture Comprehension

Choose the picture that goes with the sentence.

Circle the picture of children flying kites.

a   b   c   d

✳ Summary & Listening Practice

Listen and fill in the blanks.

SUR2-4-08
MP3

In the ① _______, children go out to fly kites. Kites come in ② _______ colors. Kites ③ _______ have different sizes. You can see kites fly ④ _______ in the sky. The wind ⑤ _______ kites go up and down. It is ⑥ _______ to fly a kite on spring days.

5 Beautiful Flowers

 **Before You Read**

1. Do you like flowers?
2. Do you think flowers are pretty?
3. Do you have flowers at home?

Flowers have different colors. Birds and bees like their different colors. They can also see the colors from far **away**. They fly to flowers and get the **seeds**. They **drop** the seeds in different places. The seeds **become beautiful** new flowers. So birds and bees help flowers in many ways. And we can enjoy looking at beautiful flowers.

 **Word Match**

Match each word with the correct meaning.

1. **seed**	a.	not near
2. **drop**	b.	the part of a plant from which new plants grow
3. **beautiful**	c.	to let something fall
4. **become**	d.	very pretty
5. **away**	e.	to change into

✳ Reading Comprehension

Choose the correct word.

1. This story is about _______ .

    a. colors   b. flowers   c. birds

2. Birds and bees like different _______ .

    a. colors   b. seeds   c. leaves

3. Birds and bees drop the _______ in different places.

    a. flowers   b. leaves   c. seeds

4. You can tell that seeds become flowers because of _______ .

    a. birds and bees   b. colors   c. rain

✳ General Understanding

Circle T for true or F for false.

1. Flowers all have the same colors.   T   F

2. Birds and bees like one color only.   T   F

3. Flowers have seeds.   T   F

4. Seeds become beautiful new flowers.   T   F

✳ Word Practice

A Circle the correct word.

1. Some people are afraid to _______ .   [flight | fly]

2. Children _______ adults.   [become | come]

3. Be careful not to _______ the box.   [hold | drop]

4. Michael lives far _______ from here.   [away | near]

5. I want to wear _______ shoes to school.   [newly | new]

B Choose the right word from the box below.

fly	seeds	beautiful	drop

1. Flowers have _______ .

2. Birds and bees _______ to flowers to get seeds.

3. Birds and bees _______ the seeds in different places.

4. The seeds become _______ new flowers.

✳ Picture Comprehension

Choose the picture that goes with the sentence.

Circle the picture of a bird and a bee getting seeds.

a   b   c   d

✳ Summary & Listening Practice

Listen and fill in the blanks.

SUR2-5-10
MP3

Flowers are colorful. Birds and bees fly to ①_______ because of their colors. They get ②_______ from flowers. Then they ③_______ the seeds in many places. The seeds ④_______ flowers. You couldn't see ⑤_______ flowers without birds and bees.

6 Strange Animals

 Before You Read

1. Do you like animals?
2. Have you ever seen a pig before?
3. Do you think pigs are dirty or clean?

Many people **think** pigs are **dirty**. They **sleep** on wet ground. But it doesn't **mean** they are dirty. When it is hot outside, the ground is cool. Pigs also like to be clean. People clean them with water. This makes them happy. Pigs look dirty, but they are very clean animals. So their places are always clean. Pigs are really **interesting** animals.

Word Match

Match each word with the correct meaning.

1. **dirty**   a. to use your mind

2. **interesting**   b. not clean

3. **mean**   c. to rest your body and mind

4. **think**   d. holding your attention

5. **sleep**   e. to give the idea of

✳ Reading Comprehension

Choose the correct word.

1. This story is about _______.

    a. animals　　　b. pigs　　　c. chickens

2. Pigs like to sleep on wet _______.

    a. ground　　　b. grass　　　c. floor

3. When people clean pigs, they are _______.

    a. sad　　　b. angry　　　c. happy

4. You can tell that pigs like _______ weather.

    a. hot　　　b. rainy　　　c. cool

✳ General Understanding

Circle T for true or F for false.

1. Many people think pigs are clean.　　　T　F

2. Pigs sleep on grass.　　　T　F

3. Pigs like to be clean.　　　T　F

4. People wash pigs with water.　　　T　F

✳ Word Practice

A Circle the correct word.

1. My friend _______ good pies.　　　[makes | uses]

2. I laugh when I am _______.　　　[happy | cry]

3. I like to sit outside when it is _______.　　　[funny | cool]

4. Clean your car! It is very _______.　　　[clean | dirty]

5. I _______ my face every morning.　　　[wash | brush]

B Choose the right word from the box below.

cool	think	wet	dirty

1. Pigs often sleep on _______ ground.

2. The wet ground is _______.

3. People _______ pigs are dirty.

4. Pigs look _______, but they are clean.

✳ Picture Comprehension

Choose the picture that goes with the sentence.

Circle the picture of the pigs.

a   b   c   d

✳ Summary & Listening Practice

SUR2-6-12
MP3

Listen and fill in the blanks.

Pigs like to ①_______ on wet ground. So people ②_______ pigs are dirty. But pigs are ③_______. They sleep on wet ground to keep ④_______. Pigs like to be clean. They are ⑤_______ when people wash them with water.

7 Amazing Animals

 ### Before You Read

1. Do you like horses?
2. Can you ride a horse?
3. Do you know what horses eat?

All horses sleep **standing** up. They have strong bones in their legs and feet. The strong bones stop them from **falling** over. Horses can stand for a very long time. They are always ready to run **fast** in case of **danger**. They are very **smart** animals. And they are also very strong animals. So horses are amazing animals in many ways.

Word Match

Match each word with the correct meaning.

1. **smart**	a. harmful situation
2. **fall**	b. to be in a position on one's feet
3. **stand**	c. moving at great speed
4. **fast**	d. very clever
5. **danger**	e. to drop from a higher place to a lower place

✳ Reading Comprehension

Choose the correct word.

1. This story is about _______.

    a. horses   b. strong bones   c. running

2. Horses have strong bones in their _______.

    a. legs   b. hands   c. back

3. Horses can stand for a _______.

    a. short time   b. long time   c. minute

4. You can tell that horses don't sleep _______.

    a. deeply   b. at all   c. standing up

✳ General Understanding

Circle T for true or F for false.

1. All horses can sleep standing up.   T   F

2. Horses fall over easily.   T   F

3. Horses are always ready to run fast.   T   F

4. Horses are not very smart.   T   F

✳ Word Practice

A Circle the correct word.

1. The train is very ________. [clever | fast]

2. My friend likes to ________. [run | slowly]

3. Many men are ________. [strong | strongly]

4. I don't like to wait in ________ lines. [long | short]

5. Can you ________ up? [lie | stand]

B Choose the right word from the box below.

strong	fall	fast	stand

1. Horses have ________ bones in their legs.

2. Horses can ________ for a long time.

3. Horses don't ________ over easily.

4. Horses can run ________.

 Picture Comprehension

Choose the picture that goes with the sentence.

Circle the picture of a horse sleeping.

a

b

c

d

 Summary & Listening Practice

Listen and fill in the blanks.

SUR2-7-14
MP3

All horses ①________ up when they are sleeping. They don't ②________ over because they have strong bones. They are ready to run very ③________ in case of ④________. Horses are very ⑤________. They are ready to run even when they are sleeping.

8 A Happy Family

 **Before You Read**

MP3
SUR2-8-15

1. Do you like to go to the zoo?
2. What kind of animals can you see at the zoo?
3. Do you know what lions like to eat?

Lions like to live **together**. In a lion **family**, you can see one **male** lion and many **female** lions. In most families, female lions look for food. The male lion looks after the other lions. Lions are big and strong animals. They **help** each other when they are in danger. They are a good family, don't you think? And they are also a happy family.

 **Word Match**

Match each word with the correct meaning.

1. **together**		a.	being a man or a boy
2. **family**		b.	with each other
3. **help**		c.	being a woman or a girl
4. **male**		d.	to make something easier for someone
5. **female**		e.	a group of people living together

✳ Reading Comprehension

Choose the correct word.

1. This story is about _______.

   a. families   b. big animals   c. lions

2. _______ lions usually look for food.

   a. Father   b. Mother   c. Old

3. Lions are big and _______.

   a. strong   b. tall   c. weak

4. You can tell that male lions look after _______.

   a. food   b. baby lions   c. themselves

✳ General Understanding

Circle T for true or F for false.

1. Lions live together as a family.   T   F

2. Father lions look for food.   T   F

3. Mother lions look after their families.   T   F

4. Lions are small animals.   T   F

✳ Word Practice

A Circle the correct word.

1. _______ dogs are bigger than female dogs. [Tall | Male]

2. Can you _______ me with my homework? [help | hurt]

3. We go to school _______ every day. [together | sit]

4. We _______ in an apartment. [like | live]

5. Lions are _______ animals. [big | small]

B Choose the right word from the box below.

help	together	big	female

1. Lions like to live _______ .

2. Lions like to _______ each other.

3. There are many _______ lions in one lion family.

4. Lions are _______ and strong.

✳ Picture Comprehension

Choose the picture that goes with the sentence.

Circle the picture of a mother lion looking for food.

a b c d

✳ Summary & Listening Practice

Listen and fill in the blanks.

SUR2-8-16
MP3

Lions ①________ together. They like to stay ②________. There is one ③________ lion and many female lions in one lion ④________. Lions are big and strong. ⑤________ help each other when they are in danger.

9 A Story of Fire

 **Before You Read**

1. Is fire hot?
2. Can children play with fire?
3. What color is a fire truck?

SUR2-9-17
MP3

People started to use **fire** a long time **ago**.
But nobody knows the **true** story about how
it happened. Many years ago, somebody **told** a story about
a small bird. It took fire from the sun and gave it to people.
Today, we use fire for many things. We can use fire to cook
food. Fire also keeps us **warm**. It was very important to people
a long time ago. Fire is still important to us now. Without fire,
we cannot live well. It really helps us in lots of ways.

 Word Match

Match each word with the correct meaning.

1. **true**   a. just a little hot

2. **warm**   b. to make known by speaking

3. **tell**   c. real

4. **ago**   d. the heat and light made by
                      something burning

5. **fire**   e. before now

✳ Reading Comprehension

Choose the correct word.

1. This story is about the beginning of _______.

   a. fire　　　　　b. the sun　　　　　c. a bird

2. The bird took fire from the _______.

   a. moon　　　　　b. people　　　　　c. sun

3. People use fire to stay _______.

   a. warm　　　　　b. cold　　　　　c. cool

4. You can tell that people need _______ to cook food.

   a. wood　　　　　b. water　　　　　c. fire

✳ General Understanding

Circle T for true or F for false.

1. Everyone knows the true story about fire.　　T　F

2. A bird took fire from the sun.　　T　F

3. The bird gave fire to animals.　　T　F

4. Today, we don't use fire.　　T　F

✳ Word Practice

A   Circle the correct word.

1. New classes _______ on Monday.   [start | cook]

2. It is very _______ in here. Let's open the window.

        [cold | warm]

3. People lived in caves a long time _______.   [ago | later]

4. Tom _______ presents to Sue every Christmas.

        [gives | goes]

5. Watch out! _______ is hot.   [Ice | Fire]

B   Choose the right word from the box below.

ago	warm	important	fire

1. People started to use fire a long time _______.

2. Today we use _______ for many things.

3. Fire keeps us _______.

4. Fire is _______ to us.

✳ Picture Comprehension

Choose the picture that goes with the sentence.

Circle the picture of a bird taking fire from the sun.

a   b   c   d

✳ Summary & Listening Practice

Listen and fill in the blanks.

SUR2-9-18
MP3

① _______ is very important to people. They started to use it a long time ② _______. But no one knows the ③ _______ about how it happened. We use fire for many things, such as keeping us ④ _______. Fire was ⑤ _______ to people, and it still is.

 10 Story Time

 Before You Read

SUR2-10-19
MP3

1. Do you like to read stories?
2. Do you like to listen to bedtime stories?
3. What is your favorite story?

Children like to hear **stories**.
They like to hear **funny** stories.
Those stories make them laugh. They
enjoy listening to stories. Parents tell stories
to their children. Sometimes the stories are about other
families. Other times they are about people who lived in the
past. Night is their favorite part of the day. Parents also
enjoy telling stories to children. So stories are important to
both parents and children.

Word Match

Match each word with the correct meaning.

1. **story**	a.	the time before now
2. **funny**	b.	a tale or description of events
3. **past**	c.	making you laugh or smile
4. **enjoy**	d.	the two together
5. **both**	e.	to like doing something

✳ Reading Comprehension

Choose the correct word.

1. This story is about ________.

   a. telling stories   b. children   c. parents

2. Children like to hear ________ stories.

   a. cold   b. funny   c. weather

3. Parents tell children stories about other ________.

   a. families   b. countries   c. toys

4. Telling stories at bedtime helps children go to ________.

   a. school   b. sleep   c. play

✳ General Understanding

Circle T for true or F for false.

1. Children like to hear stories.   T   F

2. Parents tell stories to their children.   T   F

3. Children don't like to hear bedtime stories.   T   F

4. Parents don't like to tell stories.   T   F

✳ Word Practice

A Circle the correct word.

1. Children _______ to eat ice cream.   [like | look]

2. Teachers _______ stories in class.   [talk | tell]

3. Can you _______ the birds singing?   [help | hear]

4. It was a _______ movie. I laughed a lot.   [funny | sunny]

5. Let's _______ ourselves.   [enjoy | sleepy]

B Choose the right word from the box below.

tell	stories	like	funny

1. Children like to hear _______ stories.

2. Parents _______ stories to their children.

3. Children like to hear bedtime _______.

4. Children and parents _______ story time very much.

✳ Picture Comprehension

Choose the picture that goes with the sentence.

Circle the picture of story time.

a   b   c   d

✳ Summary & Listening Practice

SUR2-10-20
MP3

Listen and fill in the blanks.

Children ①_______ hearing many stories. ②_______ stories make them laugh. Sad stories make them cry. They can learn about people who lived in the ③_______. Parents like to ④_______ stories to their children. Both parents and children like ⑤_______ time.

 11 To Get Water

 Before You Read

1. Look at the picture. What is in the bucket?
2. Have you ever seen a well before?
3. How deep is a well?

Do you know what a **well** is? Do you know what a well looks like? A long time ago, people used a well to **get** water. The well went **deep** down into the ground. At the **bottom** of a well, there was water. People used a **bucket** to get the water from a well. It was also very hard to make a well. It was also very hard to get water from a well. Nowadays only a few people use wells. This is because we have other ways to get water. But wells tell us interesting stories about the past.

✳ Word Match

Match each word with the correct meaning.

1. **well**   a. to gain; to receive

2. **deep**   b. a large container with a handle

3. **get**   c. the lowest part of something

4. **bottom**   d. a deep hole made in the ground

5. **bucket**   e. going down a long way

✳ Reading Comprehension

Choose the correct word.

1. This story is about ________.

   a. water   b. the ground   c. wells

2. At the bottom of a well, there was ________.

   a. water   b. food   c. sand

3. It was very ________ to get water from a well.

   a. hard   b. fun   c. easy

4. You can tell ________ were very important to people in the past.

   a. grass   b. buckets   c. wells

✳ General Understanding

Circle T for true or F for false.

1. People used wells to get water.   T   F

2. At the bottom of a well, there was sand.   T   F

3. It was very easy to get water.   T   F

4. Some people still use wells today.   T   F

✳ Word Practice

A Circle the correct word.

1. Don't _______ the machine. It's broken.   [use | put]

2. Tom, _______ your books. They are in your room.

     [let | get]

3. There is no water in the _______.   [bucket | smile]

4. There is a hole at the _______ of my bag.   [over | bottom]

5. The test was very _______.   [hard | hear]

B Choose the right word from the box below.

bucket	hard	deep	wells

1. A well goes _______ down into the ground.

2. You use a _______ to get water.

3. It was very _______ to make a well.

4. Some people still use _______ today.

 Picture Comprehension

Choose the picture that goes with the sentence.

Circle the picture of a person getting water from a well.

a

b

c

d

 Summary & Listening Practice

Listen and fill in the blanks.

SUR2-11-22
MP3

In the past, people used wells to ①________ water. Wells were very ②________ in the ground. There was water at the ③________ of a well. You can use a ④________ to get the ⑤________ from a well.

 **Before You Read**

SUR2-12-23
MP3

1. What time do you wake up in the morning?
2. What time do you go to bed?
3. Do you wear a watch?

There is a **special** place in England. You can see big stones standing on the ground. The stones have been there for a very long time. Some people **put** the stones on the ground. The sun came up over the stones. Every day, the sun came up in a different place. The stones told people many things. They were like **clocks** to them. The stones were very **useful** to people. They told the English many useful things. So these **large** stones were very important to them.

✳ Word Match

Match each word with the correct meaning.

1. **special**		a. an object that shows time
2. **clock**		b. to set in position
3. **large**		c. different from the rest
4. **useful**		d. big; being more than average size
5. **put**		e. good for a certain job

✳ Reading Comprehension

Choose the correct word.

1. This story is about _______ .

   a. the sun   b. England   c. stones telling time

2. There are big _______ standing on them.

   a. boxes   b. stones   c. buildings

3. The stones were like _______ to the people.

   a. stars   b. sunshine   c. clocks

4. You can tell that a long time ago _______ were very important to the people.

   a. stones   b. animals   c. plants

✳ General Understanding

Circle T for true or F for false.

1. There are big stones standing on the ground.   T   F

2. The stones were there for a short time.   T   F

3. The moon came up over the stones.   T   F

4. The stones told people many things.   T   F

✳ Word Practice

A Circle the correct word.

1. Can you _______ the cup on the table?   [put | pick]

2. The teacher _______ us to go home.   [take | told]

3. People waited in line for a very _______ time.

    [long | wrong]

4. Let's _______ a movie tonight.   [say | see]

5. Dogs are _______ to blind people.   [useful | use]

B Choose the right word from the box below.

put	special	large	useful

1. There is a _______ place in England.

2. Some people _______ the stones on the ground.

3. The stones were _______ and heavy.

4. The stones were _______ to people.

✳ Picture Comprehension

Choose the picture that goes with the sentence.

Circle the picture of a stone that tells time.

a　　　　　　　b　　　　　　　c　　　　　　　d

✳ Summary & Listening Practice

Listen and fill in the blanks.

SUR2-12-24
MP3

There are large stones standing on the ground. Some people ①________ the stones there. They were like ②________ to the people. They told the people what ③________ it was. They also told the people other ④________ things.

2

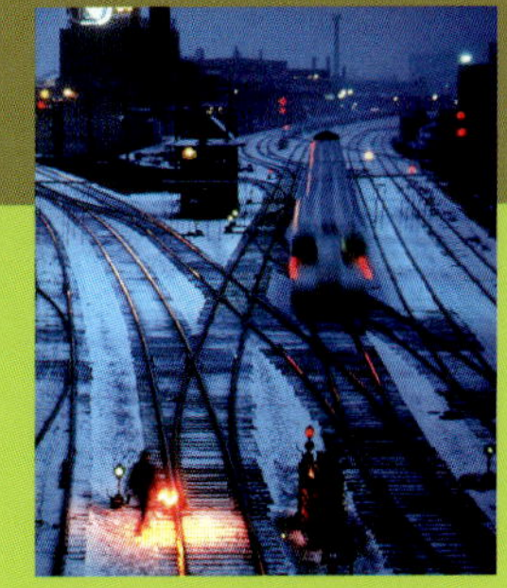

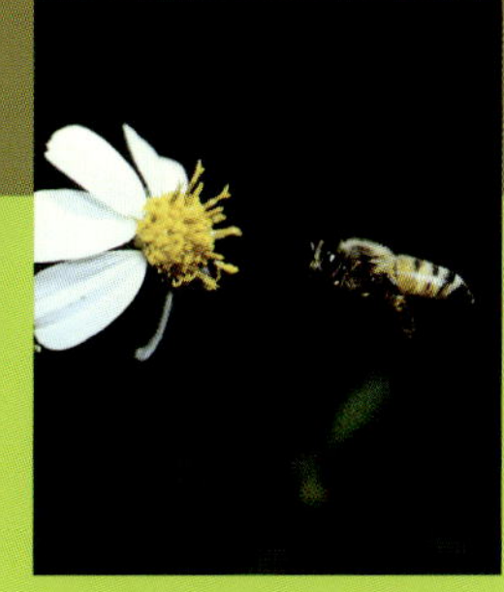

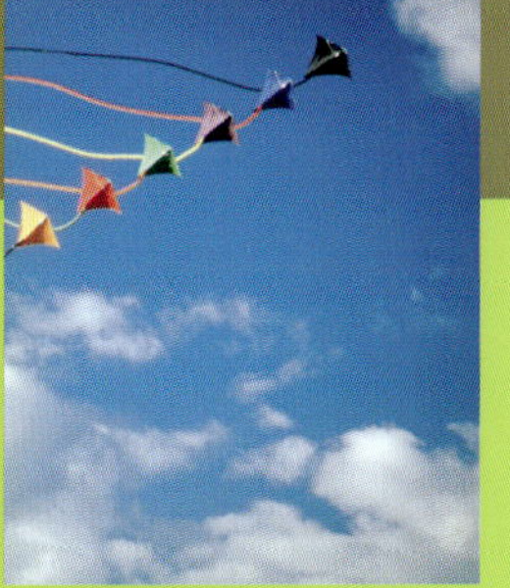

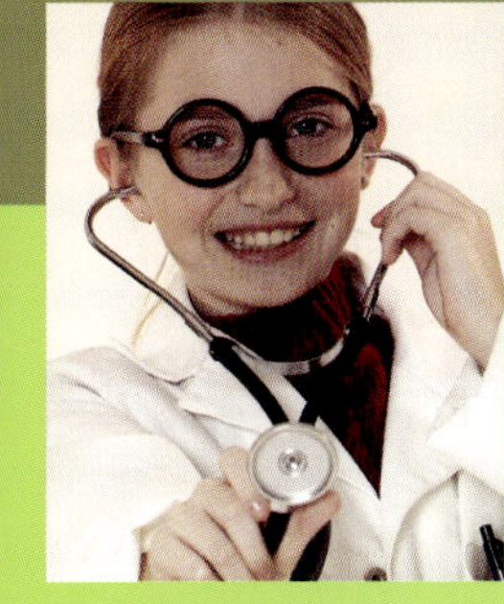

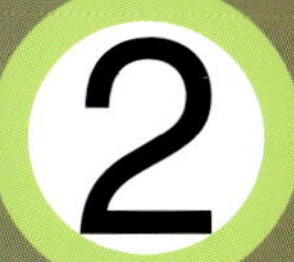

StartUp Reading

Workbook

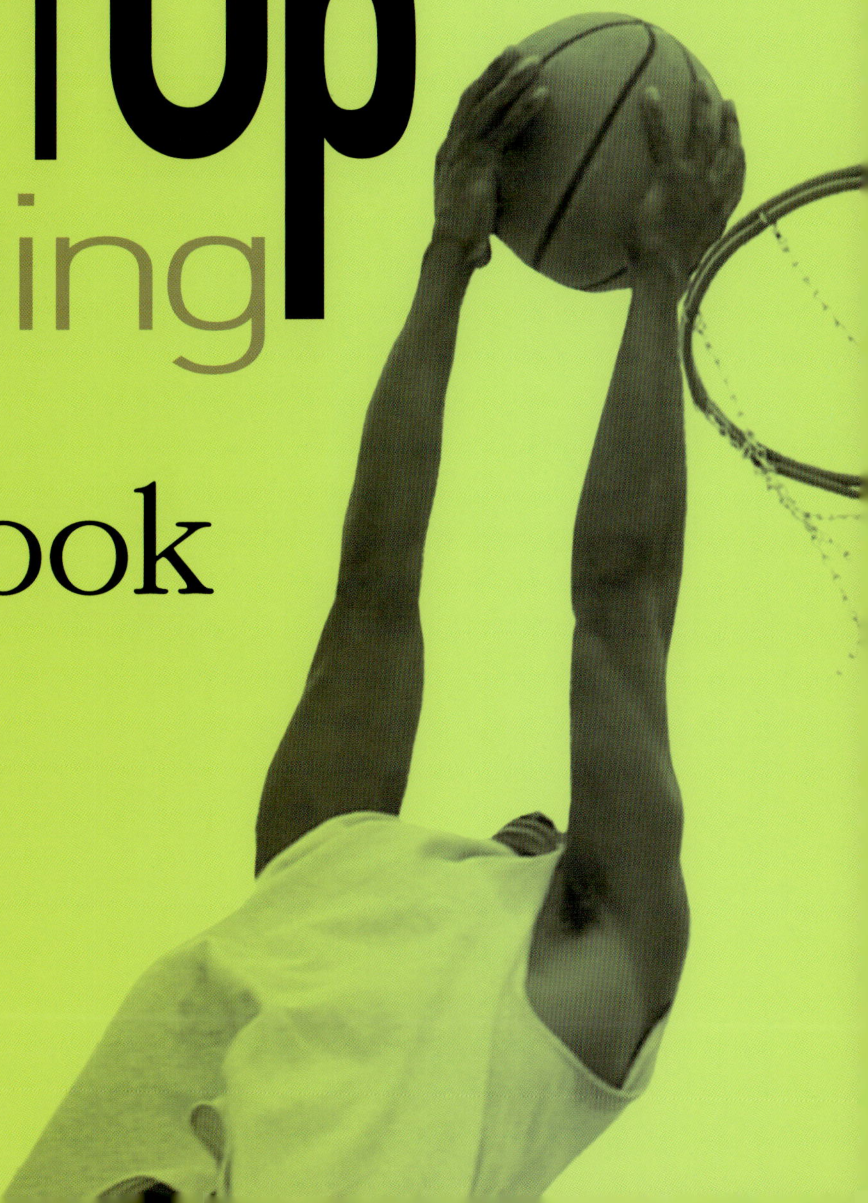

WorldCom ELT

✳ Vocabulary

New words to know

sandy   *adj.* covered with sand
Ex. Sandy places are very hot.

too   *adv.* more than is needed
Ex. Kevin's sweater is too big.

move   *v.* to go from one place to another
Ex. I'll move in to a new house this weekend.

during   *prep.* through the whole time
Ex. Sue didn't go to school during the summer.

wait   *v.* to stay in a place
Ex. Please wait for me. I'm coming.

until   *conj.* up to a certain time
Ex. We didn't fall asleep until the sun came up.

find   *v.* to look for something
Ex. Would you help me find my earrings?

rain   *v.* to fall as rain
Ex. It rains a lot in the summer.

sometimes   *adv.* not all the time
Ex. Tim goes to the park sometimes.

clever   *adj.* able to learn and understand easily
Ex. My dog is very clever.

Listening

SUR2-1-01
MP3

A Listen to the dialog and choose the best answer.  **WB** 25

1. What is the conversation about?

    a. Animals that live in cold places

    b. Animals that live in sandy places

    c. Animals that live in sunny places

2. What is true about the conversation?

    a. Animals can find food when it is still light.

    b. Animals can find food when it is sunny.

    c. Animals can find food when it is dark.

3. What is true about the boy?

    a. He asks the girl why the animals are great.

    b. He asks the girl why the animals are cute.

    c. He asks the girl why the animals are small.

B Listen and write the words you hear. **WB** 26

1. Some animals ___________ in hot ___________.

2. Animals ___________ how to ___________ food.

3. They have ___________ rain in ___________ places.

4. Plants give ___________ to animals.

5. Some ___________ are very ___________.

✳ Vocabulary Review

A What does the underlined word mean in each sentence?

1. <u>Sometimes</u> animals cannot find food.
   a. not all the time   b. never   c. always

2. Nobody likes to <u>wait</u> in line.
   a. to leave a place   b. to work in a place
   c. to stay in a place

B Choose the one word that best fits each sentence.

1. It is too cold to ____________ outside.
   a. going   b. goes   c. go

2. Some animals move when it is ____________.
   a. dark   b. darkly   c. darkness

3. It ____________ a lot in the summer.
   a. rains   b. rain   c. raining

✳ Writing

Put the words in the correct order.

1. sandy / in / Many / live / places / animals

   ____

2. hot / are / sandy / Some / very / places

   ____

3. Animals / it / until / to / is / find / food / dark / wait

   ____

✳ Vocabulary

many   *adj.* a large number or amount of
Ex. *There are many dogs at the pet store.*

people   *n.* more than one person
Ex. *How many people will come to the party?*

   prep. through the whole time
Ex. *During the summer holidays, we went swimming.*

cook   *v.* to heat food before eating it
Ex. *We will cook dinner tonight.*

fix   *v.* to repair something
Ex. *You need to fix the broken radio.*

road   *n.* a way between places which people can walk or drive on
Ex. *Turn left at the next road.*

put out   to make a fire stop burning
Ex. *Put out the campfire before you go, please.*

hard   *adj.* not easy
Ex. *The question was very hard.*

happy   *adj.* not sad; feeling good; pleased
Ex. *I am happy to see you.*

city   *n.* a large town
Ex. *This is a very beautiful city.*

 Listening

SUR2-2-03
MP3

A Listen to the dialog and choose the best answer. 📄 **WB** 27

1. What is the conversation about?

   a. The boy's father   b. The boy's mother

   c. The girl's father

2. What is true about the conversation?

   a. The boy sounds happy.   b. The boy sounds good.

   c. The boy sounds sad.

3. What is true about the boy?

   a. He sees his father all the time.

   b. He does not see his father very often.

   c. He never sees his father.

B Listen and write the words you hear. 📄 **WB** 28

1. Different ____________ have different ________________.

2. There are ____________ different jobs in the ________________.

3. People can ____________ many things at ________________.

4. It is ____________ to ____________ English.

5. We are ____________ to see you.

✴ Vocabulary Review

A What does the underlined word mean in each sentence?

1. Can you <u>fix</u> this computer?
   a. to put   b. to repair   c. to build

2. It is very <u>hard</u> to master English.
   a. not funny   b. not easy   c. not difficult

B Choose the one word that best fits each sentence.

1. When do they ___________?
   a. sleeps   b. sleeping   c. sleep

2. They take ___________ of sick people.
   a. care   b. cares   c. cared

3. The city ___________ many different people.
   a. needing   b. need   c. needs

✴ Writing

Put the words in the correct order.

1. at / people / work / Many / night

   ____

2. people / These / the / day / during / sleep

   ____

3. it is / Sometimes / to / work / at night / hard

   ____

✳ Vocabulary

New words to know

some
adj. A certain amount or a number
Ex. He needs some money.

well
adv. in a good way; very much
Ex. You speak English very well.

or
conj. used in a list of choices; if not
Ex. You can buy beef, lamb or fish.

read
v. to look at written words
Ex. The child can read and write.

through
prep. from one side to the other
Ex. We drove through the center of London.

light
n. the energy from the sun, a lamp, etc.
Ex. The light was too strong.

clear
adj. easy to see, hear or understand
Ex. His voice was not very clear on the telephone.

glasses
n. two lenses in front of your eyes to help see better
Ex. My sister has to wear glasses.

very
adv. extremely; used to make meaning stronger
Ex. I am very hungry.

important
adj. having great value or power; very necessary
Ex. This job is very important to me.

 Listening

SUR2-3-05
MP3

A Listen to the dialog and choose the best answer.  **WB** 29

1. What is the conversation about?

   a. Buying glasses   b. Wearing glasses

   c. Making glasses

2. What is true about the girl?

   a. She can't swim well.

   b. She can't see well.

   c. She can't run well.

3. What does the sign say?

   a. Walk   b. Thanks   c. Danger

B Listen and write the words you hear. **WB** 30

1. Not ____________ people can see ____________ .

2. ____________ helps us ____________ things.

3. Glasses ____________ people in many ____________ .

4. Light ____________ very ____________ to people.

5. Some people ____________ glasses all the ____________ .

✴ Vocabulary Review

A What does the underlined word mean in each sentence?

1. This picture is not so <u>clear</u>.
   a. easy to play   b. easy to see
   c. easy to use

2. Can you <u>read</u> the newspaper?
   a. to build something large   b. to look at written words
   c. to take care of something

B Choose the one word that best fits each sentence.

1. Many people can't _____________ well.
   a. reads   b. reading   c. read

2. It makes pictures _____________.
   a. clear   b. clearly   c. clearness

3. Glasses _____________ very important.
   a. are   b. is   c. am

✴ Writing

Put the words in the correct order.

1. a picture / see / by the light / We / made

   ____

2. is not / The / picture / some / people / for / clear

   ____

3. the / clearer / picture / Glasses / make

   ____

✳ Vocabulary

New words to know

kite   *n.* a toy which is flown in the air
Ex. He is flying a kite right now.

spring   *n.* the season of the year between winter and summer
Ex. Flowers bloom in spring.

different   *adj.* not the same
Ex. My bag is different from yours.

color   *n.* different effects of the light, making red, blue, green, etc.
Ex. Her favorite color is pink.

high   *adv.* far above the ground
Ex. He kicked the ball high into the air.

sky   *n.* the space above the earth
Ex. The sun is already high in the sky.

wind   *v.* a strong movement of air
Ex. There was a strong wind blowing.

make   *v.* to create; to build; to produce
Ex. I am making this hat for you.

side   *n.* one of the surface of something
Ex. We live on the other side of the road.

fun   *n.* pleasure and enjoyment
Ex. We had a lot of fun at the party.

 Listening

SUR2-4-07
MP3

A Listen to the dialog and choose the best answer. WB 31

1. What is the conversation about?

   a. Singing a song   b. Flying kites

   c. Playing football

2. What is true about the conversation?

   a. They will study.   b. They will play tennis.

   c. They will fly kites.

3. What is true about the girl?

   a. She likes to study music.

   b. She likes to play.

   c. She likes to teach children.

B Listen and write the words you hear. WB 32

1. Many __________ like to __________ kites.

2. There are many different __________ of kites.

3. The wind helps __________ __________ many ways.

4. __________ of the wind, you can fly __________.

5. The __________ can __________ kites in many ways.

 Vocabulary Review

A What does the underlined word mean in each sentence?

1. I want to fly <u>high</u>.
   a. a long way up   b. a long way down
   c. from side to side

2. She's such a <u>pretty</u> girl.
   a. nice to look at   b. nice to hear   c. nice to touch

B Choose the one word that best fits each sentence.

1. Kites can ___________ in many ways.
   a. moved   b. moving   c. move

2. You can see kites ___________ from side to side.
   a. goes   b. go   c. went

3. Many children like to fly kites in ___________.
   a. winter   b. spring   c. summer

Writing

Put the words in the correct order.

1. are / kites / others / big / are / Some / small

   ____

2. come in / Kites / colors / pretty / also

   ____

3. You / the wind / fly / cannot / without / a kite

   ____

✳ Vocabulary

flower   *n.* the colored part of a plant or tree
Ex. This colorful flower grows well.

bird   *n.* a creature with feathers and wings that can fly
Ex. Birds can fly fast.

bee   *n.* a black and yellow insect
Ex. Bees make sweet honey.

get   *v.* to receive or buy; to have
Ex. Did you get a present from your mother?

seed   *n.* the part of a plant from which new plants grow
Ex. Put the seed in the ground.

become   *v.* to come to be
Ex. My sister became a doctor.

way   *n.* how something is done; method
Ex. What is the best way to study?

beautiful   *adj.* very pretty or attractive
Ex. He has a beautiful voice.

enjoy   *v.* to be pleased or satisfied by something
Ex. I enjoy reading good books.

near   *adj.* not far; close to
Ex. Let's walk. The shop is quite near.

 Listening 

SUR2-5-09
MP3

A Listen to the dialog and choose the best answer. WB 33

1. What is the conversation about?

   a. Roses   b. The girl   c. Flowers

2. What is true about the conversation?

   a. The girl does not know where flowers come from.

   b. The girl does not think that flowers are beautiful.

   c. The girl thinks that flowers are the same as seeds.

3. What is true about the boy?

   a. He does not think that flowers are beautiful.

   b. He knows where flowers come from.

   c. He does not like flowers.

B Listen and write the words you hear. WB 34

1. There are __________ different __________ of flowers.

2. Birds and __________ help __________ bloom.

3. __________ are quite different __________ flowers.

4. Seeds are __________ in many places.

5. Flowers __________ us smile.

✳ Vocabulary Review

A What does the underlined word mean in each sentence?

1. These flowers are so <u>beautiful</u>.
    a. very ugly   b. very heavy   c. very pretty

2. <u>Drop</u> the gun now!
    a. to let something fall   b. to let something fly high
    c. to let something go from side to side

B Choose the one word that best fits each sentence.

1. Birds and bees ____________ flowers.
    a. likes   b. like   c. liking

2. Birds can ____________ high.
    a. flies   b. fly   c. flying

3. Look at this ____________ flower!
    a. newness   b. newly   c. new

✳ Writing

Put the words in the correct order.

1. have / colors / different / Flowers

    ____

2. drop / different / They / the seeds / places / in

    ____

3. new / become / flowers / The seeds / beautiful

    ____

✳ Vocabulary

New words to know

pig	*n.* a fat pinkish animal with short legs and a short tail *Ex. A pig is a farm animal.*
dirty	*adj.* not clean *Ex. Your hands are dirty. Go and wash them!*
ground	*n.* land; the earth's surface; soil *Ex. He fell to the ground.*
mean	*v.* to give the idea of *Ex. The red light means "stop."*
outside	*adv.* in, at or to a place that is not in a room or building *Ex. Please wait outside a few minutes.*
with	*prep.* using; having *Ex. He fixed it with a tool.*
water	*n.* the clear liquid without color, smell or taste *Ex. I'm thirsty. Give me some water, please.*
look	*v.* to turn the eyes toward something; to seem to be *Ex. He looks like a movie star.*
always	*adv.* at all times; every time *Ex. You are always late. What's wrong with you?*
really	*adv.* in fact; very much *Ex. I am really tired.*

 Listening

SUR2-6-11
MP3

A Listen to the dialog and choose the best answer. MP3 **WB** 35

1. What is the conversation about?

   a. Cleaning your room   b. Animals

   c. Pigs

2. What is true about the boy?

   a. He does not like pigs.   b. He likes pigs very much.

   c. He does not like the girl.

3. What is true about the conversation?

   a. Pigs are dirty animals.   b. Pigs are clean animals.

   c. Pigs are beautiful animals.

B Listen and write the words you hear. MP3 **WB** 36

1. Many people ____________ like ____________.

2. Pigs are not ____________ when it is ____________.

3. Pigs are happy when it is ____________.

4. Water can ____________ pigs.

5. Pigs ____________ like to ____________ clean.

✳ Vocabulary Review

A   What does the underlined word mean in each sentence?

1. When do you <u>sleep</u>?
   a. to move your body
   b. to rest your body and mind
   c. to change your mind

2. The <u>ground</u> is very dirty.
   a. surface of the earth   b. the clear liquid
   c. surface of the water

B   Choose the one word that best fits each sentence.

1. Pigs like to ___________ on the ground.
   a. sleep   b. sleeps   c. sleeping

2. Cool weather makes pigs ___________ .
   a. happy   b. happily   c. happiness

3. You look so ___________ . What happened?
   a. dirtiness   b. dirty   c. dirtily

✳ Writing

Put the words in the correct order.

1. ground / on / sleep / wet / Pigs

   ____

2. clean / water / with / People / them

   ____

3. really / animals / Pigs / interesting / are

   ____

✳ Vocabulary

New words to know

amazing *adj.* very surprising and difficult to believe
Ex. She shows amazing courage.

horse *n.* a large animal that is used for riding
Ex. A young horse is a foal.

stand *v.* to be on your feet, not sitting or lying down
Ex. They were standing near the window.

leg *n.* one of the parts of the body on which a person or animal stands or walks
Ex. A spider has eight legs.

feet *n.* plural of foot
Ex. Put the socks on your feet. It is cold outside.

stop *v.* to finish moving
Ex. My watch stopped.

fall *v.* to drop down toward the ground
Ex. The rain was falling steadily.

fast *adv.* quickly; moving or working at great speed
Ex. She ran very fast.

in case because something might happen
Ex. I will take an umbrella in case it rains.

smart *adj.* clever; intelligent
Ex. He is not smart.

✳ Listening

A Listen to the dialog and choose the best answer. 📄 WB 37

1. What is the conversation about?

    a. Pigs   b. Horses   c. Cows

2. What is true about the boy?

    a. He thinks that horses are cute.

    b. He loves horses.

    c. He does not think that horses are nice.

3. What is true about the conversation?

    a. Horses are very weak.   b. Horses are very strong.

    c. Horses are very dirty.

B Listen and write the words you hear. 📄 WB 38

1. Horses have very ___________ bones.

2. When in __________, horses can run very ___________.

3. ___________ are very, very ___________.

4. Horses can __________ for many ___________.

5. Horses are amazing ___________ lots of ways.

✳ Vocabulary Review

A What does the underlined word mean in each sentence?

1. Children can be very <u>smart</u>.
    a. very young   b. very clever   c. very old

2. Watch out! We're in <u>danger</u>.
    a. safe situation   b. good situation
    c. harmful situation

B Choose the one word that best fits each sentence.

1. Your strong bones stop you from ____________ over.
    a. fall   b. falls   c. falling

2. We're ready to ____________ you.
    a. helps   b. help   c. helping

3. Horses can sleep ____________ up.
    a. stands   b. standing   c. stand

✳ Writing

Put the words in the correct order.

1. sleep / All / horses / up / standing

    ____

2. very long / for / a / can / Horses / time / stand

    ____

3. smart / animals / They / very / are

    ____

✳ Vocabulary

family   *n.* the group that includes children and their parents
Ex. I have a large family.

lion   *n.* a large animal of the cat family
Ex. A young lion is called a cub.

together   *adv.* with each other
Ex. Can we have lunch together?

male   *adj.* being a man or a boy
Ex. There are some male nurses here.

female   *adj.* being a woman or a girl
Ex. I want to get a female cat.

most   *adj.* nearly all of a group of people or thing
Ex. Most people in this country have pets.

food   *n.* something that people or animals eat
Ex. Have you tried Korean food?

look after   to take care of somebody or something
Ex. She looks after her children when she's not at work.

each other   used to show that each of two or more people does something to the other or others
Ex. We looked at each other.

think   *v.* to produce thoughts; to believe
Ex. Do you think we will win?

 **Listening**

SUR2-8-15
MP3

A Listen to the dialog and choose the best answer. MP3 WB 39

1. What is the conversation about?

   a. Lions   b. Horses   c. A family

2. What is true about the boy?

   a. He thinks that lions are cute.

   b. He thinks that lions are dirty.

   c. He thinks that lions are amazing.

3. What is true about the conversation?

   a. The girl does not like lions.

   b. The boy hates lions.

   c. Lions do not help each other.

B Listen and write the words you hear. MP3 WB 40

1. Lots of ___________ live ___________.

2. There are many ___________ lions in ___________ lion family.

3. Lions help ___________ other.

4. Everybody ___________ to have a happy ___________.

5. Lions are ___________ and ___________.

✳ Vocabulary Review

A What does the underlined word mean in each sentence?

1. Shall we work <u>together</u>?
    a. alone   b. by yourself   c. with each other

2. We're a happy <u>family</u>.
    a. a group of people who hate each other
    b. a group of animals fighting with each other
    c. a group of people living together

B Choose the one word that best fits each sentence.

1. Female lions ____________ for food.
    a. look   b. looks   c. looking

2. People like to ____________ together.
    a. living   b. lives   c. live

3. Male lions look ____________ other lions.
    a. before   b. after   c. behind

✳ Writing

Put the words in the correct order.

1. like / to / together / live / Lions

    ____

2. look for / In / female lions / food / families / most

    ____

3. help / other / each / when they / They / in danger / are

    ____

✳ Vocabulary

New words to know

fire *n.* the heat and light produced by something burning
Ex. Firemen put out the fire.

start *v.* to begin; to make something begin
Ex. What time do you start work?

know *v.* to understand something as correct
Ex. Give me a chance. I know the answer.

true *adj.* right or correct; real or genuine
Ex. Is it true that he is leaving?

about *prep.* having relation to
Ex. We will talk about the weather.

small *adj.* not large in size
Ex. She has a small car.

sun *n.* the huge star in the sky that provides heat and light to earth
Ex. The sun rises in the east.

take *v.* to carry something; to seize; to capture
Ex. I will take the yellow pencil.

ago *adv.* in the past; back in time from now
Ex. I met him a long time ago.

lots of many; much; a lot of
Ex. You need lots of friends.

✳ Listening

SUR2-9-17
MP3

A Listen to the dialog and choose the best answer. WB 41

1. What is the conversation about?

    a. Fire   b. Time   c. Somebody

2. What is true about the conversation?

    a. A long time ago, people did not use fire.

    b. We know how people started to use fire.

    c. People started to use fire a long time ago.

3. What is true about the boy?

    a. He knows how people started to use fire.

    b. He likes the girl very much.

    c. He does not know how people started to use fire.

B Listen and write the words you hear. WB 42

1. Many ____________ happened a long ____________ ago.

2. I have a very interesting ____________ to ____________.

3. ____________ helps people do ____________ of things.

4. Without fire, we cannot ____________ food.

5. Fire is ____________ to us.

✳ Vocabulary Review

A What does the underlined word mean in each sentence?

1. Is that <u>true</u>?
   a. real b. ready c. rich

2. I want to live in <u>warm</u> places.
   a. a little cold b. just a little hot c. cool

3. Do you know how to <u>cook</u>?
   a. to buy food b. to make food c. to like food

B Choose the one word that best fits each sentence.

1. Nobody ___________ the answer.
   a. know b. knowing c. knows

2. People ___________ to cook a long time ago.
   a. started b. start c. starts

3. It will keep you ___________ .
   a. warm b. warmly c. warmth

✳ Writing

Put the words in the correct order.

1. a / long / started / use / to / ago / time / fire / People

   ____

2. told / a / Somebody / about / bird / story / a / small

   ____

3. to / It / people / gave / fire

   ____

✳ Vocabulary

funny   *adj.* making you smile or laugh
Ex. He is very funny.

laugh   *v.* to make the sounds that express happy feelings
Ex. You always make me laugh.

listen   *v.* to try to hear
Ex. Now please listen carefully.

parent   *n.* a person's mother or father
Ex. Parents take care of their children.

past   *n.* the time gone by; the time before now
Ex. I know nothing about his past.

bedtime   *n.* the time that you go to bed
Ex. He bought me a bedtime book.

favorite   *adj.* liked more than others of the same kind
Ex. What is your favorite food?

part   *n.* one of the pieces, areas or periods
Ex. Which part of Korea do you come from?

tell   *v.* to give information
Ex. I will tell you later.

both   *det.* used to talk about two people, things, etc. together
Ex. Both girls were French.

 **Listening**

SUR2-10-19
MP3

A Listen to the dialog and choose the best answer. .MP3 **WB** 43

1. What is the conversation about?

   a. Favorite part of the day   b. Favorite flower

   c. Favorite day of the year

2. What is true about the boy?

   a. He does not like his parents.

   b. He does not enjoy listening to stories.

   c. Bedtime is his favorite part of the day.

3. What is true about the conversation?

   a. The girl likes the boy very much.

   b. The boy's parents tell him interesting stories.

   c. The girl's parents tell her interesting stories.

B Listen and write the words you hear. .MP3 **WB** 44

1. We have interesting ___________ to tell.

2. Funny stories ___________ people ___________.

3. Parents ___________ telling stories ___________ children.

4. Stories are ___________ many different things.

5. Stories help ___________ in lots ___________ ways.

✳ Vocabulary Review

A What does the underlined word mean in each sentence?

1. Do you <u>enjoy</u> reading books?
    a. to stop doing something   b. to begin doing something
    c. to like doing something

2. Isn't that a <u>funny</u> story?
    a. making you laugh   b. making you cry
    c. making you sick

B Choose the one word that best fits each sentence.

1. Children like to ___________ funny stories.
    a. hears   b. hear   c. hearing

2. Parents enjoy ___________ children stories.
    a. tell   b. tells   c. telling

3. Many different people ___________ in the past.
    a. live   b. lives   c. lived

✳ Writing

Put the words in the correct order.

1. like / stories / hear / Children / to

____

2. stories / Sometimes / are / families / other / about / the

____

3. their / favorite / is / Night / the day / of / part

____

✳ Vocabulary

New words to know

well   *n.* a deep hole in the ground
      Ex. It is an oil well.

deep   *adj.* going far down
      Ex. The lake is very deep.

bottom *n.* the lowest part of something
      Ex. The house is at the bottom of a hill.

bucket *n.* a round, open container
      Ex. How many buckets of water do you need?

nowadays *adv.* at the present time
      Ex. I don't go there nowadays.

because *conj.* for the reason that
      Ex. They didn't go out because it was raining.

gain   *v.* to win or obtain something
      Ex. I gained weight a lot.

container *n.* a box, bottle, packet, etc.
      Ex. She bought a plastic container.

handle *n.* the part of an object that you use for holding or
      opening it
      Ex. She turned the handle and opened the door.

hole   *n.* an opening; an empty space
      Ex. There are holes in my socks.

 Listening

SUR2-11-21
MP3

A Listen to the dialog and choose the best answer. MP3 WB 45

1. What is the conversation about?

    a. Boys   b. Wells   c. Animals

2. What is true about the girl?

    a. She thinks that wells are bad.

    b. She thinks that wells are amazing.

    c. She thinks that wells are cold.

3. What is true about the conversation?

    a. People got water from a picture.

    b. People got water from the sky.

    c. People got water from a well.

B Listen and write the words you hear. MP3 WB 46

1. In the past, many people ____________ a well to ____________ water.

2. People need ____________ to ____________ well.

3. People used a ____________ to get water.

4. There are many ways to ____________ water.

5. Wells ____________ water in them.

✳ Vocabulary Review

A What does the underlined word mean in each sentence?

1. There was a hole at the <u>bottom</u> of the shoe.
   a. the highest part   b. the middle part
   c. the lowest part

2. There was a monster <u>deep</u> inside the cave.
   a. going up a long way   b. going down a long way
   c. going out to sea

B Choose the one word that best fits each sentence.

1. Do you know what she __________ like?
   a. look   b. looking   c. looks

2. They __________ to the park yesterday.
   a. go   b. going   c. went

3. It __________ very hard to find water.
   a. was   b. were   c. are

✳ Writing

Put the words in the correct order.

1. what / you / a / Do / know / is / well

   ____

2. The / ground / deep down / went / well / into / the

   ____

3. people / a few / only / Nowadays / use / wells

   ____

✳ Vocabulary

New words to know

stone	*n.* a hard, solid substance *Ex. The house was built of grey stone.*
like	*prep.* similar to something or somebody *Ex. Do it like this.*
clock	*n.* an instrument that shows you what time it is *Ex. I need an alarm clock.*
useful	*adj.* helpful; having some practical use *Ex. It is a useful tool.*
large	*adj.* greater in size and amount than usual *Ex. I'd like a large coffee, please.*
machine	*n.* a piece of equipment with moving part *Ex. This is a washing machine.*
watch	*n.* a type of small clock *Ex. My watch is a bit slow.*
size	*n.* how big or small something is *Ex. What size shoes do you need?*
position	*n.* the place where something is *Ex. My legs hurt, so I changed position.*
wrong	*adj.* not right or correct *Ex. You've got the wrong number.*

Listening

SUR2-12-23
MP3

A Listen to the dialog and choose the best answer.  **WB** 47

1. What is the conversation about?

   a. Special stones   b. Special time   c. Special friends

2. What is true about the conversation?

   a. The stones are in France.

   b. The stones told people many things.

   c. The stones are not special at all.

3. What is true about the girl?

   a. She thinks that the stones are amazing.

   b. She thinks that the stones are bad.

   c. She thinks that the stones are too cold.

B Listen and write the words you hear. **WB** 48

1. There are ___________ stones ___________ England.

2. Some ___________ stones are ___________ on the ground.

3. Who ___________ the stones on ___________ ground?

4. The sun came up ___________ the stones ___________ day.

5. The ___________ are ___________ to ___________ .

35

✳ Vocabulary Review

A What does the underlined word mean in each sentence?

1. Some places are very <u>special</u>.
    a. the same as the rest   b. usual
    c. different from the rest

2. This watch is very <u>useful</u> to me.
    a. good for a certain job   b. bad for a certain job
    c. different from others

B Choose the one word that best fits each sentence.

1. There _____________ many things in the room.
    a. are   b. is   c. was

2. In the past, those stones _____________ people many things.
    a. tell   b. tells   c. told

3. The stones were _____________ clocks.
    a. likes   b. like   c. liked

✳ Writing

Put the words in the correct order.

1. stones / You / big / on the ground / standing / can / see

    ____

2. The sun / over / stones / the / came up

    ____

3. things / told / many / people / The stones

    ____